The

SECRET
SIGNATURE
of THINGS

The

SECRET
SIGNATURE
of THINGS

EVE
JOSEPH

Brick Books

Library and Archives Canada Cataloguing in Publication

Joseph, Eve, 1953-
    The secret signature of things / Eve Joseph.

Poems.
ISBN 978-1-894078-81-8

    I. Title.

PS8619.O84S43 2010   C811'.6   C2009-907382-X

We acknowledge the Canada Council for the Arts, the Government
of Canada through the Book Publishing Industry Development
Program (BPIDP), and the Ontario Arts Council for their support
of our publishing program.

   Canada

The cover image is a photograph taken by Patrick Friesen.

The author photograph was taken by Saul Joseph.

The book is set in Minion and Grotesque.

Design and layout by Alan Siu.

Printed and bound by Sunville Printco Inc.

Brick Books
431 Boler Road, Box 20081
London, Ontario N6K 4G6

www.brickbooks.ca

For Patrick

I am carried in my shadow
like a violin
in its black case.

– Tomas Tranströmer

Contents

MENAGERIE

AMONGST STRANGERS

A FEW PROVISIONS

TRACKING

MENAGERIE

Crow

I have no song.

Think consonants –
hard beads
at the back of my throat.

Think black fan
snapped open.

It was raven
who stole the sun,
not me.

Think Hasidim,

barefoot
on a sandy beach.

Carp

Hiroshige caught me,

lidless
hallucinatory.

I wear my finest
kimono
the sleeves sway
easily.

Tattooed with mother
of pearl,
hard bony light,

stitch and overlay,
the work of it –

I, too, long
for my love's return.

Violet-Green Swallow

So this is what
             it's like –

feint, tilt,
        swoop

and glide –

to return as bird

and not some other creature
                finned or clawed.

Too quick for my shadow –

above the trees

                I return
as
        script.

Golden Retriever

I'm content
curled at the feet

of the old men sitting at their tables
in the sun. They talk

about what went wrong
after a strong season, pause

at the sound of high heels, and then
resume; they reach down

absent-mindedly –
I am a vague memory

of grass and mud and the dirty tricks
that boys will play on boys.

On and on they go
deeper into the past –

like them,
I dig things up

and bury them
again.

Drone

Summers, I imagine
so much more
than the sound
      of my own falling.

Heads of flowers dip,
they swallow me whole –
the scent overpowers.

What boy doesn't wish
to disappear
so completely?

I brush against
their sex. I am
their golden boy.

Green Frog

Throat singer
of the pond –

I am a soloist
in the night choir.

Put aside the things of winter:
wind, snow, sleet –

soon a chorus will rise.
Listen –

sly as absinthe, a green army
slides in among the rushes.

Rock Pigeon

Barred from the temple,
filth does not offend me.

In your parks, among your statues,
there is something of Europe in me.

Late afternoon, old women
shuffle across the square.

We part, a blue-green sea
at their feet:

Are you lonely? we say,
coo, rooc'too coo.

You are lovely, we say,
coo rooc'too coo coo.

Spider

I cast out silk
like a fisherman casts
out his line
landing the fly.

To the delirious
I appear
climbing the cream-coloured wall.

Suspended

over the sickbed
I am
a small black emissary
from the land of sickness
and sometimes

death.

Cormorant

Hung-over,
standing around with the boys,

a bridegroom in a rumpled
black suit.

Wings to the sun,
wings to the wind –

I want to sing
like the great Caruso

at the Savoy Hotel.

Sea Turtle

for Saul

Tend to my wounds,
   return me
      to the sea.

The necropsy
   will tell you nothing
      of white sands, violet light,

of what it was
   to carry a seabird
      on my back,

to be a small island,
   solitary,
      to have wheeled

amongst the stars
   reflected on the waters
      above me.

AMONGST STRANGERS

Old Age

It surprises me each time
I see a horse lie
down in a field

        a protest

in the bend and
fold, the way a body
relinquishes its hold as it
sinks, unguarded,
to the earth.

Dugout

It took two of us
to flip the canoe
from where it lay
all winter in the yard.
Beneath its fire-bellied bulk
grass had grown bright yellow
in patches long, then short.
All winter
riding the waves
in the golden summer sun.

Fog

This morning I felt the fog
before I saw it
hanging itself like gauze over the arbutus

and making what is close
unattainable. For one moment I believed
I smelled eucalyptus, my feet

dusted with fine motes of sand.
I must have journeyed in the night,
returned to a seaside village

where light is compromised
by particles of water, although the mist
has a certain density one can trust,

a weight I can gauge
relative to wind: a dampness capable
of penetrating clothing, skin, sometimes

loneliness. I woke this morning
to the absence of foghorns, unable to sustain
even the most inadvertent holiness.

Convalescence

Pears and Camembert,
tea with honey, long afternoons

spent reading
in an armchair in the sun.

The grounds at Villa Grimaldi
lovingly tended by the ones who don't forget;

the instruments of torture
rendered impotent.

The voice of doubt stilled
for the moment –

long afternoons and the body
sinking into itself.

In the bloody fields of battle,
the great horses grazing.

Passage

In the wake of the ship
whole forests fell silent;
green gave way to gold
as we sailed, farther
each day from home.

We cut our way
across the flight path of albatross,
through schools of flying fish,
and waited for something to arrive –

seabirds, fishing boats,
junks with their Venetian sails.
A sign to interpret, any sign at all.

We sailed as if we were the first
to carry such a cargo
over so great a distance.

I was a young woman in love
with nothing. Looking back
I see that between what I was
and what I would become
were those places that cast me out.

Do not read too much into this:
for brief periods I entered
my own life and rejoiced
at what I found there.

The ship is not a metaphor

although it could be –
we sailed from Ocean Falls to San Francisco,
from Puerto Cabello to Caracas,

I was twenty, what I knew of the world
did not include the ports or the whores waiting there,
the country bars or the boys selling their sisters
on the streets of Acajutla.

There was the sea. Between ports, there was the sea.

Calypso Orchids

She misjudged
the weather again,
went out in
a thin green cardigan.

The little
mountain orchids
shivered to see
her dressed so foolishly.

Styawat

for Leigh

All summer you watched the clouds.
Shapes shifted: swans turned into fish,
winged horses plunged through white drifts.

Shadows moved across the ground.
Impossible to know fact from myth –
all summer you watched the clouds.
Shapes shifted, swans transformed into fish.

Your grandfather remembers a time when salmon
walked out of the river as men. Your small face lifts;
You are the wind that brings the sun, he whispers.
All summer you watched the clouds,
shapes shifted, men turned into fish,
winged horses plunged through white drifts.

Translation

In one translation of Akhmatova
a few early snowflakes blow in the wind
barely, barely.

In another –
same wind, same early flakes – only
lightly, lightly.

Was she thinking about winter, or
the stranger at the door?

It matters that water never stopped moving
beneath the frozen canals

and lips that barely brushed hers
were not the ones she lightly kissed.

White Camellias

The poems that don't get written get up before dawn to work in the cannery, hands slippery with slime and scaled in silver.

In the lunchroom they listen to The Pointer Sisters singing *I want a man with a slow hand* and talk about the villages they left and how, when the fish stop running, they'll head down to Washington and pick raspberries for the Japanese man.

Their children squealing and filling the flats quick as nickels flipped through the air.

They like sockeye season best, the firm red meat of it. Laughing, calling themselves fish widows, slipping their knives down the backbone, they reminisce about their men sitting up all night at the river like shepherds with their long gaff poles.

The smokehouses full to the rafters with Indian candy.

All night dogs barked in the valley.

One poem thought it was the deer stepping out of winter to lick the salt grass. Another believed it was the old songs agitating the dogs –

casting a net around the dead, pulling them closer.

One hurled huge boulders across the Cheakumus River Valley
marking the boundaries along the Elaho, Clendenning –

all the way to Payakentsut.

The ones I don't write argue with those who maintain there is no
difference between *mind* and *brain*.

They have stored the mind's explorations in the brain's vault –

they have watched the river rising, parting around the pylons of
the stone bridge, urgent in a way it wasn't a few days ago, rising
from sigh to murmur, agitated on its way to the falls.

These ones know the brain is only the cartographer intricately
mapping what the mind explores.

As if there was ever a way to return.

One got drunk with nine sailors in San Francisco
                    and woke up with a tattoo on her ankle.

※

Another watched brightly painted fishing boats lowered
                                    hand over hand
down the cliffs of Manarola into the Gulf of Poets.

※

The poems I don't write tire easily of metaphor –
to them, the sea is just the sea and the owl a bird and not some
messenger of death.

※

Some are shy –
damaged like young girls whose mothers were good women
                            incapable of love.

Like actors with stage fright, they dread the moment the curtain
opens fearing no words will come or, if they do, they will belong to
someone else.

※

In Buenos Aires, one appeared as a man dancing alone on the streets of La Boca. Arms wrapped around an invisible partner.

Another disguised itself as a young girl doing cartwheels along the canal in Trieste in a thin white dress spun by spiders.

A third hovered between here and there; at night she slept with the window open, in the morning her pillow was snow.

❧

These poems have walked the streets of some other poet's city. They have felt the muscle and sinew, the brutality of all that is common.

3:00 a.m., wide awake again. Convinced the train is lost in the mountains, the long whistle sent out like a homing signal. A cry of distress. My children asleep six hundred miles away.

They too, are not written.

❧

Yesterday it snowed on and off all morning.

The North Shore Mountains rename themselves:
>   *The Lions, The Sisters, Sleeping Beauty.*

The unwritten ones, too, take on new and unfamiliar shapes.

❧

The ashes of one are scattered in the harbour. At night the water
is darker than I imagined, the city lonelier.

Lights from the grain elevators undulate on the water, I'm uneasy
driving over Second Narrows Bridge. Under floodlights, a freighter
unloads its cargo. By morning it will be gone as if it never existed.

Some things are still too fresh. Rain fell on her cold face –
there was so much I wanted to ask but never thought to.

❧

Carried away with it all, one believed itself to be Lorca
and dreamed 100 lines about white camellias
>   and sorrowful blue guitars.

❧

Some have held me in their arms, stroked my hair and loved me
like a daughter. They have blown out the candles and covered the
mirrors at the time of their death.

🌿

Those I don't write are loyal like all broken things.

They have thrown themselves nightly on their loved ones' graves
                              and stayed there until morning.

They have heard bells ringing and voices chanting in the old
language invoking *Jesus* and *Mary* and felt serpents writhing
in their bellies and ghosts hitchhiking on their backs.

They have sat in straight-backed chairs
                  as the hands of the healers moved over them like air.

Creation

Spend it all, says Annie Dillard:

the black-capped chickadees –
       dart and song of those quick bandits;

the bike ride earlier today
past the few remaining gladiolas –

naples yellow, dog-tongue pink,
hues of fuchsia.

See how the crow is nothing like his cousin,
       that trickster with his
scorched wing.

Open the box,
       go ahead –

watch the stars burn small holes
in the tent
beneath which
       we all bed down.

The Language of Birds

after Galway Kinnell

If one were to interpret the language of birds
one might begin by confessing a fear
of heights, remembering days atop
the hemlock and the uneasy alliance of
thin branch beneath feet; and one would
have to study landings, carefully, for many,
many years before attempting to fall
with arms wide open from some great height.
If one were to interpret the language of birds.

If one were to interpret the language of birds
one would have to throw open the doors
and let them all in: warbler, wren, the swift river swallow,
and it would be necessary to make a bed
in the girders beneath the silver train bridge
and in the rafters of the abandoned barn
where the farmer hanged himself
and the swallows sang him all night from flesh.
If one were to interpret the language of birds.

In order to interpret the language of birds
one must ask what the crow knows of death,
what the red-winged blackbird knows of the reed
in the marsh where the world begins, again,
each morning, and one must rise out of bed
although the desire to do so is gone and the grey light
falling through the window touches, briefly,
a sadness that lives inside all that one is,
in order to interpret the language of birds.

If one were to interpret the language of birds
it would be necessary to steal from other songs
the one true song – the few notes sung
to please the jailor – and in singing feel
bones begin to thin and throat lengthen
and like the Baal Shem Tov one would hear
their entreaties and know their songs
as the first griefs ever sung.
If one were to interpret the language of birds.

On Beginning

i

Despite Lorca's arsenic lobster.
Neruda drunk with the great starry void.
Despite the air above Jerusalem
heavy with prayers – Amichai's
muse and marrow of form, light and geometry –
      the angel ruffling one's hair.

Despite Whitman and the beautiful uncut hair of graves.
Despite a mind of winter,
a woman sitting at the night window,
snow falling and branches like broken wings
hanging from the cypress.

Despite the gravy of ten good years, blue light
washing over the body,
despite the dancer, the singer,
                the sweet, sweet swing of it,
the torero relinquishing form and technique,
tossing his heart over the bull's horns
                  over and over again.

Despite the tight, dry seal of oneself.

ii

Before precision, before the first cut,
                              it begins –

wood before it is mask, horn before it is rattle.

At daybreak, it starts in the crossover –
that moment
              the frogs hand the day over to the birds.

It begins in breakage, Glück's dark compliment
                              to the art of making.

Sshh, it says,
              sshh,

there now, begin.

On Schedule

4:00 a.m.
the train's whistle
a single note –
      long and cavernous
unwinding
      somewhere off in the mountains.

The 4:37 bird answers
with pertinacious song –

like someone learning to whistle,
pushing air out of pursed lips

(*little sister to big brother:*
      see! see!)

      auditioning, auditioning

to be the one
      to bring on the dawn.

Amongst Strangers

The voice of the Polish poet lingers in the room;
it's not his words that remain but the places
that spread out before them –

hilltops overlooking conquered villages.
Settlements, tent cities, shantytowns,
the temporary shelters and long trips upriver.

What lingers is the notion
that one has a beloved city
to return to in this life –

not a promise of salvation
but a place, here, amongst strangers
where the seats of the train station

are worn and polished like pews
and the streets occupied
with the commerce of old acquaintance.

Siwash Rock

for Salia

Sing to me, she said, sing me the name
of the man turned to stone. Again
and again remind me of the hero –
and what it is I need to know
about currents and tides in this burial place.

What of the mask and the moon's blue face?
Where do you go when you go far away?
Here where the river meets up with the sea, oh
sing to me, Papa, the story of water.

Am I not your beautiful daughter?
Sing me to sleep, sing me awake,
teach me to see the shape of the old
in the haze of the city and all of your ghosts –
is it true that we're made of rubies and clay?
Stay with me Papa –
           sing me oh sing me
                  the very first names.

Benevolence

The seeds
you fed the birds
to ward off winter

sprouted.

Bird grass
you called it.

In those,
your last days,

a late benevolence
revealed itself;
what was not scattered
grew to nourish us.

What was no longer useful,
the wind carried away.

You Crossed in Winter

for Ian

You crossed in winter,
the train's whistle hollow –
a sharp splinter

of sound across the Narrows.
Memory, involuntary prayer,
blazes through heart into marrow:

it was said you had a flair –
brief, bright
sparks flying in the midnight air,

small fires in the sky.
You loved the north,
the Dew Line spread out like

a pearl necklace against a frozen throat.
What's left is strange, fantastic –
a white kingly hand and you holding court

drunk, beautiful, unfit.
Unable to fly, you crossed
this country in a sky-blue casket.

Boy

If I could
I would give him
a border collie,
black with a white chest,
a dog so loyal it would come
to his voice only.
I would take the bullets
out of his father's gun.

If I could
I would be the reach
in the singer's voice,
the note breaking
between hymn and cry –
indecipherable.

If I could
I would give him the light
in the room where his father lay dying,
the barn door flung open,
thirty swallows,
one blue horse.

A Brief Visit

In his last weeks he called out
the names of the dead.

Most often it was a kind of greeting,
the way one might leave the gate
to the garden open, or
the chair pulled slightly back
from the table.

Occasionally he seemed surprised
by the peripheral dead, the ones
spoken about in hushed tones
in the stunned days of summer.

I didn't know him.
I was only there at the time
of his dying, the short hour
before his death.

What I saw was this:
his wife bent over him
whispering the names of the dead,
throwing open the gate
to let them all in.

.

Halfway World

In the halfway world of the Pantanal,
aquatic and terrestrial
ghosts, stars and fireflies
everywhere.
Night smelling of ripe fruit,
lilies, dirt roads.
Breathing it all in,
visitors,
the two of you
like moss green birds,
exotic and endangered.
The indigenous people
gone,
the children stolen.
Prepare to listen to
the Truth and Reconciliation Commission
at home –
the stories of unmarked graves
waiting to be told.
Not knowing what's ahead.

How will the dead speak?

Not knowing what's ahead,
waiting to be told
the stories of unmarked graves
at home.
The Truth and Reconciliation Commission
prepares to listen to
the stolen children –
gone
the indigenous people,

exotic and endangered
like moss green birds.
The two of you
visitors,
breathing it all in –
lilies, dirt roads
night smelling of ripe fruit.
Everywhere
ghosts, stars and fireflies
aquatic and terrestrial
in the halfway world of the Pantanal.

A FEW PROVISIONS

Signs

Are we drawn from sleep like fresh well water surfacing, hand over hand, into the morning light? Or do we stand in the doorway watching the guests as they leave in their various disguises? Either way, we leave one place behind and arrive at another.

Some dreams, I'm told, are visits; others, old problems working themselves out. I envy those without doubt, the ones who find comfort in the appearance of a hummingbird in winter or an eagle circling above a freshly dug grave. I looked for you on a remote beach, a crow hopped near the surf, another watched from a twisted arbutus; as much as I wanted to believe, I remembered how much you hated crows.

It's not easy looking for a sign; hoping for a pinwheel of light to spin in the middle of the night or a woman in a long white dress to finally appear. Sometimes I think I'm too stubborn to see you, rejecting everything you offer as proof: your address on a random licence plate, a favourite song playing in the doctor's office, "A Nightingale Sang in Berkeley Square," or perhaps something else by Vera Lynn; and what was I supposed to think about the bees, hundreds of them spilling out of the flowers in the chapel and the one lying motionless on the pillow in the morning?

Sometimes a voice singing in one room breaks a heart in another. A figure crosses an empty square where hours ago a bride stepped into her new life; sometimes a voice sweeps across a tiled city lifting scrap and leaf, calling a name, the same name over and over. The doorway is empty. Impossible to say if somebody once stood there and waved.

Questions

I want to ask poetry where it was for all those years. Where was it when I chain-smoked my way through Vancouver bingo parlours and where was it when I traded my Penguin classics for True Crime stories? I want to ask about waitressing in Chinese restaurants and slinging beer in Indian bars and about hitchhiking and smoking dope and seeing the prairies for the first time. I want to ask about underground rivers and the homelessness of rain and how it knows what it knows and why it knows so much more than I do. I want to ask poetry where it goes when it disappears and if it was there when I shot pool and crashed in cheap hotels in small towns across the country. I want to ask it why it drew me close and then let go and if it led me to the dying as a way of keeping me alive. I want to know how it found me on a red bench in a mountain cemetery and if it slept beside my daughter in a graveyard full of lost boys in Eilat. I want to ask if it appeared one day as an albatross weaving across our wake and, if so, was it the Mariner's bird or was it mine? Did it appear another time as a young girl dancing alone at night on a seawall in Riomaggiore? Did it travel with me like the tip of a blind man's cane as I stumbled into my life? I want to know about blindness. I want to ask poetry where the birds went when they disappeared and how it was they reappeared in cursive loops like a new language above the daffodil fields one afternoon in late March.

Instructions

They say if you are going to burn food for the dead you must do so
before 3:00 p.m. when they begin to wander and you can't separate
the good ones from the bad or the lonely from the lost. If you must
cry, then cry before sunrise when the world is still asleep and the
fallow deer of James Island can be seen emerging out of the forest
like shy brides. Turn in a full circle when you leave the graveyard so
they will not be tempted to follow you back to their old rooms and
start up again with their irritating obsessions.

Walk once more to your mother's grave. Lift the thin metal loop,
push open the gate. Inside the graveyard snow will have fallen all
night. A second burial. Only this time she will speak to you: *this way*,
she will say, *this way*, past the trails left by invisible mourners, past
the crow who followed her all the way home. Forget the old stories,
the ones your mother couldn't shake. Remember she was a tango, a
fox trot, a slow waltz before the music stopped.

Listen instead to the language of owls. Pause, your key in the door;
they will return you to the night. Let them show you, with their black
shadows, a blacker silhouette. Light slips through a crack beneath
your door. A call sweetens the night. Do not assume they are coming
for you. Do not assume they are death.

Arrhythmia

I hear, as if from a great distance, the sound of a clock on my bedside table. It is beating sixty ticks a minute and my heart is keeping perfect rhythm. I feel, briefly, the deep even pulse of my blood for the first time in a month.

Who knows why the heart misfires, skips a beat and then can't find its way back. Like the skipping game we played as girls: *high, low, jolly, slow, salt, sugar, mustard, pepper*! Miss a beat and you were out.

In one day the blood travels 12,000 miles: the distance from New York to Nagano, the number of miles a gray whale travels each summer on its way to feast on ghost shrimp and herring eggs. On clear nights we see the satellites orbit the heavens 12,000 miles above the surface of the earth.

In the early 1600s, William Harvey wrote: *the blood is moved perfected, made vegetable, and is defended from corruption.* In bed I feel the uncorrupted, vegetable flow of it through my entire body.

When I was a child I cupped an injured bird in my hands. Its one good wing beat frantically against my palms. One month ago I woke to my heart fluttering in my chest cavity. One good wing beating. Sparrows often flew into our windows. In our house we put injured birds in cardboard boxes with holes punched in the lids. My friend put the ones she retrieved in paper bags where fifty percent of them recovered. I buried most of mine in the backyard; she watched some of hers fly out of brown bags. The cardiologist tells me there is a fifty-fifty chance my heart will return to atrial fibrillation once I stop taking flecainide and diltiazem.

Da Vinci believed the heart was of such density that fire could scarcely destroy it.

Like the earth's hum we hear the heart only when we stop and listen. In a recent echocardiogram I heard the wet thwump of it; on the screen bursts of red and green static pulsed with every contraction. To my eyes the heart looked like a weather map with one hell of a big storm on the radar.

Lately, I've become aware of its erratic knocking. A bit like having a drunk at the wheel.

Who knows why the heart misfires? The cardiologist says it has to do with age. The mystic believes the heart wants to leave, wants to hear its voice reverberate through the valley. For once, it wants to beat as the one heart of the world, to light whole cities with its circuitry, to swagger through the mountains with the ancestor of thunder and his attendants of rain.

The human embryonic heart starts beating approximately three weeks after conception: we are older than our hearts by 21 days; in the end however they often outlive us, firing on for seconds, sometimes minutes, after our last breath.

So many last beats. The man who sat up all night waiting for death to approach. The woman who cried for the heads to be chopped off all the flowers in case the smell of earth, rain, jasmine held her back; in case the morning light, afternoon sun, the neighbour's dog barking at nothing called to her as she was leaving. The ones who died alone. The ones I have forgotten.

One of the ways to return the heart to regular rhythm is to shock it with defibrillator paddles; another is to slow it down with drugs. Like rebooting a computer. The first time I was given adenosine, my heart went from 180 beats a minute to 20; the second time it stopped for four seconds. One minute the engines were full throttle, the next I was in a glider; conscious, coasting in a silent body.

Not long ago, a dry exhalation ripped through the sky. In bed I felt my heart circle and drag between strikes, composing in a rhythm all its own, trading the metronome for the musical phrase.

In the storm's violet light, it wants to follow that wild music.

Canoe Builder

Porch lights have come on all down the street. In front of one of the houses a white cat sleeps on a pillow in a dugout hollowed by fire. If you could look back, you'd see an old man tending that fire. You'd hear the river talking to the stones, the grass shrugging off the wind. The smell of red cedar would put you to sleep. You'd see a dog tied to the clothesline with a long leash and a colossal log drying in an old shed. The old man has nothing to do with magic but that doesn't stop the carved bear from rocking or the feast dish from dancing. He offers you bread and jam at his table with the blue and white plastic tablecloth. He gives you a new name. It's late. You haven't stayed up like this for a long time. It is a kind of visit. He didn't come to you; you had to go to him. The dead, you realize, are preoccupied with winter. The river will freeze. All of us will need a sturdy boat, a few provisions. Each time he pokes the fire it bites down hard: when you look up you can't tell stars from sparks.

Thief

Once again it's disappeared. You go looking for it on the periphery of town. Summer is gone from the river; the Catholic boys jack-knifing into the water with their silver medallions have vanished. Gone, too, are the horses that pulled the wagon. It is not interested in your ideas. It is the sparrow that steals from the martin, the starling that steals from the sparrow. In one hand it holds a woman and the sea; in the other, family graveyards in tall grass. You try to reason with it, to seduce it with fire and ice, but it has its own creation stories. It has no need of yours. It walks thirty miles through the night carrying a baby in its arms, glancing over its shoulder to see who's following. It knows there are stragglers at risk of getting lost. Thieves who will steal its history and turn it into poetry.

Momentum

The boy on his bicycle thinks, *I will ride to the mountains and then to the sea.* The Chinese gardener runs behind steadying him before letting go. The boy rides through the streets of Shanghai, past the mango man with his cart crying out, *mangoes, fresh mangoes,* past the merchant selling baby ducklings, on his way to the Cossack who will teach him how to really ride, standing in the saddle. The boy thinks, *I am the emperor of this kingdom, all my subjects adore me.* His mother calls him home. At night the servant pours his bath and places three live ducklings in the water. In cafés people are uneasy; the men talk amongst themselves about war. Across the bay at Wei Hai Wei, the gunboats are insect class: Mantis, Tarantula, Gnat, Grasshopper, Cricket, Dragonfly. Names the boy catches in a jar, oblivious to the talk of curfew, the soldier kneeling down to tie his boot.

The Stranger

The woman who came close to death opens the door to her home
and walks into a room she has never set foot in. Her books are piled
neatly on a desk beside a jar of sharpened pencils. Her jacket hangs
from a hook on the back of the door. She is like the amnesiac who
marvels at her beloved possessions as they are placed in her hand one
by one but turns away from them easily once they are put down. She
makes tea with fresh mint and sits in the sun at a wooden table in
her kitchen. Outside the window a man in a black coat and top hat
is sitting in a tree swinging his feet. How will she know if he is real?
How will she know if he has come for her?

Snowdrops

Impatient with the dark, snowdrops push through the earth into
white days of winter. The first battalion to arrive at the front, they
are eager like the boy who lies about his age and signs up at sixteen.
A young nurse picks a bunch for the field hospital. To her they seem
like brides left at the altar, heads drooping on slender stems. Little
flags raised in surrender. Listen, they say, others will follow: daffodils
then tulips, grape hyacinth, iris, bluebells and larkspur. By early May,
lily of the valley will arrive, sailors return to the sea, workers rise.
The ladies of the court will kiss whom they please. Slowly the ground
will soften, war will end. There will be a brief summer before the
cold winds pick up again.

Perseverance

Late fall. In ditches, on rock slopes, along old rail lines, Icelandic poppies are the last ones standing. When all others – blackberry, thistle, scotch broom – have fallen, the delicate poppies persevere. And, like all things that go on and on, they no longer know what it is they hold on for or how it was they began. There are no obstacles to overcome, no sorrows they must endure. Unlike Nehemiah, they have no broken wall to repair around a holy city. They gather in their thin dresses like young girls at closing time. *Flamenco. Wonderland. Oregon Rainbow. Party Fun.* When all others have packed up they remain, folding slowly in on themselves, petal by petal, after the last drunk has staggered home.

TRACKING

*I need to put a human face
to what's happening...*

– from *Finding Dawn*, a film on missing aboriginal
women by filmmaker Christine Welsh

So you think you can tell…
blue skies from pain?

                        – Roger Waters

i   .   .

The city stirs in stairwells
leading down
to public washrooms

in doorways
in alleys
– exposed on the periphery

for what it is.
Trains shunt
fugitive through the night –

under massive floodlights
the goods of the city pass from
hand to hand.

Chain link and culvert
cut across
old ghost trails

downtown:
a shooting gallery
where the Green Door used to be.

ii

What is it about numbers?
One woman goes missing

then another
and another.

So many last places
like pockets of cold in a lukewarm sea,

the sudden shock leaving you breathless
as you pass through.

You didn't go looking,
the stories clung

like iron filings
as if you were a direction home.

Nothing prepared you
for the insistence of spirits –

on the cutting room floor
the ones you left behind

watch in the trees,
in the smoke.

In your hometown
the wind is bilingual –

sometimes it speaks in English,
sometimes in Cree.

iii

Your divining rod bends
in old neighbourhoods.
In the scrub and berry-tangled brush

along deserted highways
it combs through
sun-bleached grasses;

beneath mountain ash
it dives
into bright red funeral berries.

Through inlets, into the Narrows,
people and animals shift their forms;.
you search for a clue

in the stories
of water, the stories
of land.

Arm's-length apart
on the banks of the Saskatchewan
the search grid expands –

fanned out,
the hunters and trappers
scour the land.

iv

What of the ones
who vanished perfectly?

Tracks as
invisible as

a trapline in winter
the morning after fresh snowfall.

v

You've seen kitchen tables, bowls of sugar,
burnt matches stuck in crib boards, old photos
tacked on living room walls.

You've seen the command centre, the street nurses,
the Valentine's Day marches through alleys
on the downtown eastside.

You've withdrawn from the light
shining on the inner circle –
from the politics of loss.

You've been there when the women arrived,
arms full, the counters covered with platters,
pans, the forty-cup coffee urn beginning to perk.

You've heard the drums and the singers,
the women's song and the warrior's song,
the welcome songs and the songs of grass.

On a stretch of the Yellowhead
you've learned to keep the gas can filled,
your car in good working order.

vi

In the interstices
between rationality and myth,
in a forest

real or imagined,
a table consumed by fire
is the closest you come to prayer –

send them:

smoked fish and grease
fried bread and tea
send them

whiskey and dope
wild flowers and soap
send them lace bras and panties
and buckets
of berries

send more
send everything

sing
the whole time
the fire is burning.

Not the dead you feared,
but their rage,
pain without object,

formless, furious, inconsolable.
What began as story became
irrevocably altered into promise:

how, you asked, *how
do I comfort the dead?*

vii

If you called the names,
if you called each one,

where would you call her
home to?

A reserve in northern B.C.,
before that a remote village,

before that a valley, say
the Elaho,

the river white with snow,
giants watching over it all.

One year spent looking for hope
yielded precious little.

Think of it in visual terms:
what in god's name would it look like?

The bingo halls and crack pipes,
the photo, face-down in a dresser drawer,

of a girl in her Sunday clothes
smiling shyly for the camera.

Years later, a red-headed woman
standing in a boat –

returning home, returning home
to face the beast.

viii

There is no sense to be made of this,
no solace

other than the singers with their drums
standing in a circle in the gymnasium;

old songs sung
when the dead outnumbered the living,

songs that fathers and brothers
spread their arms to as they dance

like eagles over the hardwood floor.

Songs the deaf can hear.

Songs to hold up the sick
and carry them around the fire,

songs to call the missing home.

If you called each one
where would you call her home to?

No solace except in the drum
and in that one country song –

the singer with her wide-open busted heart
singing,

call my name,

singing,

is that you
and if that's you
have you always been with me?

ix

The city has overgrown itself
like a vine. Russian trade beads, copper shields –

the currency of memory
engraved on headstones

in a moss-green forest.
Things are entangled,

braided together – sweetgrass
in the chain-link fence,

in the glove compartment
of your car. Sweetgrass

meadows near the town
you grew up in.

The grass that never dies.
It's how you speak with ghosts –

in an abalone shell mixed with cedar, sage, tobacco,
the language of smoke.

x

It is said that spirits travel
on flowing water: rivers, creeks,

underground streams.
And with each death it is said

a child will arrive with memories
not yet faded from the other side.

Some of them watch over you –
have made you one of them.

You didn't know, years ago, they
wouldn't let you go.

Had you known
you might have begun hoarding

songs, prayers, incantations, red
sashes, old fiddles, saskatoons –

you might have saved pouches of tobacco
and gone to meet them alone,

four days
on the mountain
waiting,

laden
with gifts.

Waiting,
thinking:
*how do we hold them close
even as we let them go?*

Shelter

The rubber plant in the hospital cafeteria is waiting for rain. Palms
up beneath a sky of fluorescent lights, its leaves are broad enough
to be roof, temporary shelter, shade to small creatures caught in the
open. The hiker, for instance, who has made a fire with wet twigs and
hunkers down to wait it out under his wide blue tarpaulin.

Acknowledgements

My sincere thanks to the B.C. Arts Council and the Banff Centre for the Arts for their support during the writing of this book.

Thank you also to the editors of the literary journals and anthologies in which some of these poems have appeared: *Grain, The Malahat Review, Descant, Vintage 2000, The Antigonish Review, The New Quarterly, Poetry Northwest, Long Journey: Contemporary Northwest Poets 2006, Rocksalt 2008,* and *The Poets Guide to Birds 2009.* "Translation" and "Violet Green Swallow" were awarded second prize in *The Antigonish Review's* Great Blue Heron Contest 2007. "Momentum," "Canoe Builder," "Snowdrops," and "The Stranger" were awarded second prize in *The Antigonish Review's* Great Blue Heron Contest 2009. "White Camellias" won *The Malahat Review's* 2010 P.K. Page Founders' Award for Poetry.

Thanks to James Ducey for his permission to use the Santee Cave Pictograph.

I am deeply grateful to Don McKay and Barry Dempster for their generosity and love of poetry and to Chris Hutchinson for our ongoing conversation. I am indebted to Alayna Munce for her fine editing skills and friendship. Thanks to Maureen Harris, Kitty Lewis, and Alan Siu at Brick Books.

Thanks, as well, to Christine Welsh for the work that she does and for sharing a part of that work with me.

My love and appreciation to Leigh, Lee, Saul, Salia, Niko, Elisa, Marijke, and Pedro and to my love, Patrick.

Welcome Jonah.

And finally, thanks to the lfc for the wild nights and wonderful company.

Eve Joseph grew up in North Vancouver. As a young woman she worked on freighters and travelled widely before moving to Vancouver Island where she now lives with her family. Her first book, *The Startled Heart*, was shortlisted for the Dorothy Livesay Poetry Prize.